MW00973151

17 STEPS FROM ZERO TO HERO

THE SECRETS OF CHAMPIONSHIP LIVING

ALAN MUSHEGAN, JR.

17 STEPS FROM ZERO TO HERO
Copyright © 2004 by Alan Mushegan, Jr.

Unless otherwise indicated, all Scripture quotations
are taken from the Holy Bible, *New International Version*
(NIV), copyright © 1973, 1978, 1984 by the International
Bible Society. Used by permission.

Scripture quotations marked (TLB) are from
The Living Bible, copyright © 1971 by Tyndale House
Publishers. Used by permission.

Scripture quotations marked (KJV) are from the
King James Version of the Bible.

All rights reserved. No part of this publication may be
reproduced, stored in a retrieval system, or transmitted in
any form by means electronic, mechanical, photocopying,
recording or otherwise, except for the inclusion of brief
quotations in a review, without prior permission
in writing from the publisher.

ISBN: 0-9740880-3-X

Published by

LIFEBRIDGE
B O O K S
P.O. BOX 49428
CHARLOTTE, NC 28277

Printed in the United States of America.
COVER DESIGN BY JR GRAPHICS

DEDICATION

To all my friends and family at
Full Turn who have helped make
our dreams a reality.
This book is also dedicated to my father
– who has always been, and will
forever be, my hero.

Contents

INTRODUCTION

As an eight-year-old kid I loved Karate movies. There was nothing better than watching Bruce Lee – the legendary hero who made mincemeat out of the bad guys with spin-kicks and flying leaps.

"Wouldn't it be great to be just like him?" I dreamed, trying every way I could to emulate the kung-fu fighter. My obsession was to be a black belt – as high as you could go in the martial arts.

Chuck Norris, who starred in such movies as "The Karate Cop," was another favorite. When my dad took me to a personal appearance the actor made in Atlanta. I got to shake his hand. On cloud nine, I thought "This is the greatest moment of my life!"

At the age of ten I was taking classes at a local martial arts school. The sport consumed me. I would watch the best fighters and spar with the most experienced people in my class – some of them twenty years my senior. To say I was passionate about excelling is an understatement.

Not once did I fail a test that would advance me to

the next level. By the time I was 12 I had reached my dream – a junior black belt.

At that moment, however, something changed inside me. But more about that later.

What about you? Who is your hero? Perhaps it is a great author whose writings have inspired your life, your second-grade teacher who boosted your self-esteem, or a grandma who loved you unconditionally.

True heroes can impact millions or only a few, yet these exceptional individuals leave a lasting impression on every person they touch.

If you've ever watched *Survivor* on television, you know the ultimate goal is to "outwit, outlast and outplay" the competition. By contrast, in the true game of life we are not competing against someone else, but *ourselves*.

As you will discover, this book is not about choosing a hero, but *becoming* one. It is not a manual on how to win a gold medal at the Olympics or take home an Oscar at the Academy Awards. Rather, it is a step-by-step guide to championship living, regardless of the arena you choose.

My father, Alan Mushegan, Sr., one of my great heroes, drilled into me this principle: *You can only be what your desire demands.*

On these pages you will learn:

- How to keep your past from destroying your destiny.
- Where to place your focus for achievement.
- How to catch the spirit of a hero.
- What to say when people tell you, "No."
- How to tap into your secret power.
- The keys to overcoming a "zero" start.
- What your Creator says about your future.
  – plus much more.

If your heartfelt longing is to fulfill God's great expectations for your life, read on!

– Alan Mushegan, Jr.

VISUALIZE THE VICTORY!

Have you ever watched prize-winning gymnasts perform their routine? Look closely. You can almost see them go through the motions of their next move before their body springs into action.

They visualize the victory – seeing themselves in perfect form from start to finish.

Your imagination is a powerful tool. Since I was old enough to remember, I have been taught: *If you can see it, you can achieve it.*

Let's try an experiment. Right now, after reading this paragraph, I want you to get comfortable – take in a deep breath, then release it. Now imagine yourself doing something you have always wanted to do but have been afraid to try. It might be riding a horse, or speaking in front of a thousand people. Go ahead. Let your mind cross that boundary.

YOU CAN'T DEPEND ON YOUR EYES WHEN YOUR IMAGINATION IS OUT OF FOCUS

– MARK TWAIN

"*I CAN DO THIS!*"

How does it feel to see yourself accomplishing something out of your comfort zone? You've just taken the first step to reaching new heights – doing something you have never done before.

- If you see yourself failing, you will always fail.
- If you are afraid to *be*, you will never become.

Let's flip to the other side of the coin: When you picture yourself achieving the impossible, the image will become a possibility. It's not that you are deceiving yourself; you are finally realizing the abilities you have always possessed. As the Bible expresses it: *"Where there is no vision, the people perish"* (Proverbs 29:18).

> **WHEN YOU PICTURE YOURSELF ACHIEVING THE IMPOSSIBLE, THE IMAGE WILL BECOME A POSSIBILITY.**

When a view of victory is emblazoned in your brain, confidence builds. You begin to say, "I can do this! I really can!"

In the process you are exercising faith – seeing *"things that are not as though they were"* (Romans 4:17). What we visualize becomes reality because we are literally *pulling* it into existence.

Listen to your Heavenly Father's advice when He says: "Let the weak say 'I am strong.' Let the poor say 'I am rich.' "Let the blind say 'I can see.'"

Start viewing yourself as God sees you!

FAREWELL STATUS QUO

I must admit, during my early days in ministry I didn't fully comprehend the power of vision. For six years I taught a weekly class of 25 to 30 young people – content and comfortable with the familiar faces.

People would come and go, yet the size of the group remained the same.

Finally, I reached the point where I became troubled by the status quo and began to hunger for something new. In prayer, I clearly heard the voice of the Lord say, "Alan, you can double the number of young people to whom you are ministering."

Suddenly, I saw the group not only *doubling,* but *tripling,* and even more! I had a new vision, a burning passion for the youth of our area and began to imagine the room overflowing with people – and souls coming to Christ.

Inspired, that same month I gave our youth ministry a new name, *Full Turn*, to announce to the world we were going to make a complete change. I not only shared my vision with the group, but targeted lofty goals we could all work toward.

"WE'RE NEVER GOING BACK!"

Within three months the group grew from 25 to 100. There were people sitting and standing in every nook and cranny – we were bursting at the seams.

I JOYFULLY DECLARED, "WE ARE NEVER GOING BACK TO THAT CLASSROOM!"

To accommodate the rapid growth, we rented a tent. After 150 teenagers showed up the first night we began setting even larger goals. I joyfully declared, "We are never going back to that classroom!"

Soon the tent was overflowing and our church invested in a permanent building for *Full Turn*. During construction we had to move our meetings from Wednesday nights to Monday so we could utilize the church sanctuary.

Within six months our Monday night meetings climbed to 300 – then grew to over 500 in our brand

NOTHING HAPPENS UNLESS FIRST A DREAM.

– CARL SANDBURG

new facility.

This explosive growth happened because the Lord convicted me of being average. Now I wanted more – and began to *see* more. To God be the glory!

BEYOND THE PRESENT

Never allow yourself to simply go through the motions. Just because you have the knowledge and ability to function in an assignment does not mean you will excel.

Look beyond the present – to the place you long to be. See yourself becoming a financial success so you can support the work of missions. Envision the dream house in which you want to raise your family, and the kinds of friends you would like to enjoy.

> *JUST BECAUSE YOU HAVE THE KNOWLEDGE AND ABILITY TO FUNCTION IN AN ASSIGNMENT DOES NOT MEAN YOU WILL EXCEL.*

Later, we'll talk about strategies for success. As we start, however, remember that when you have a ten year goal, set a five year interim target – then break it down even further into a series of one year plans. Now *see yourself* achieving each of those steps.

YOUR MASTERPIECE

Every architect goes into a building project with a detailed set of blueprints. He conceives the completed project before the first load of cement is poured into the foundation.

A great artist will stare at a blank canvas and somehow see a masterpiece.

With God's help, your life can become whatever you dream. Visualize the victory!

FOCUS ON THE DESTINATION, NOT THE JOURNEY

T he long road named "Champion" is littered with obstacles, yet if you stay on the path and follow the proper signs, you will reach your objective.

Here's the problem. Most well-intentioned people become so caught up in the journey they never make it to their destination.

It is so easy to become sidetracked. Often, we have noble plans until something pops up to distract us. I am sure you've had an important project to accomplish, yet the task stays in limbo because your attention is diverted.

A QUICKER ROUTE?

Have you ever taken a trip and been so impatient

IN HIS HEART A MAN PLANS HIS COURSE, BUT THE LORD DETERMINES HIS STEPS.

– PROVERBS 16:9

to reach your destination you could mentally see yourself already there – having the time of your life? Maybe you were headed to the beach and pictured yourself wading in the ocean, smelling the crisp salty air, only to realize there were hours of driving still ahead?

I remember the day similar thoughts flooded my mind as I contemplated my future. I worried, "Shouldn't I be doing something else with my life?"

At the time, I was at the ripe old age of 19 and had been in youth ministry for three years. I enjoyed my work and knew this was what God had called me to do, however, I wanted to

> *"SHOULDN'T I BE DOING SOMETHING ELSE WITH MY LIFE?"*

skip ahead to bigger and better things – looking for a quicker route to my ultimate destination.

I soon learned that if I wanted to reach the finish line I was required to take the journey.

The reason few people make it to the summit is because they allow their frustrations to get the best of them. They hit a rough spot and, discouraged, give up.

Overnight successes are few and far between. If we could simply snap our fingers and realize our dream, we wouldn't need God's guiding principles.

THE PROCESS

When my father was a little boy, a friend gave him a seed to plant. He told me, "I was so excited that I immediately ran outside and buried it in the ground."

Everyday he would dig up the seed to see if it was growing. He couldn't understand why it wouldn't sprout. Much later he realized, "It never grew because I didn't give it *time* to grow."

It is human nature to look for shortcuts. As one fellow said: "I want patience – and I want it *now!*"

Every end product requires a time-consuming process. We click the remote on our TV and watch an athlete in the act of winning, failing to realize the thousands of hours spent honing his or her skills. Without exception, the person who attains great heights has paid a great price.

You can only achieve what you refuse to relinquish. If you desire something strongly enough you are well on the way to obtaining it.

Today, focus on the destination, not the journey.

STEP 3

START WITH WHAT YOU HAVE

In each of the four Gospels – Matthew, Mark, Luke and John – you will read the story of Jesus feeling such compassion for the multitude that followed Him, He miraculously fed them with five loaves of bread and two small fishes.

This miracle of multiplication was such a memorable event that each writer makes a point of mentioning there was *more* than enough: *"When they had all had enough to eat, [Jesus] said to his disciples, 'Gather the pieces that are left over. Let nothing be wasted.' So they gathered them and filled twelve baskets with the pieces of the five barley loaves left over by those who had eaten"* (John 6:12-13).

However, only one of the writers – John – tells us about an unlikely person who assisted the Lord in this great miracle. When Jesus wanted to know if any food was available, Andrew, one of the disciples, commented, *"Here is a boy with five small barley loaves and two small fish, but how far will they go among so many?"* (John 6:9)

SEIZE THE MOMENT!

The hero of the day was a young child who, in an unselfish act, offered his lunch so the Lord could feed the multitude.

We don't even have a record of his name, yet this lad played a vital role in the lives of many people. Becoming a hero does not mean you will be remembered by the masses, but it does signify that when your moment for greatness arises, you must seize it.

In that vast multitude, surely there must have been others with something to offer, yet they held back. This young boy gave all he had – and that's what led to the miracle.

"RUNNING OVER!"

After witnessing that awesome event, I'm sure many would have gladly given Jesus *anything* so they could have been part of what took place. True heroes, however, do not follow the crowd or wait to see what is working for someone else. Instead, they capture the moment – having faith the Master will perform wonders.

It is still God's desire that the work of His Kingdom be accomplished, yet it takes people of faith to carry it out. If you need a miracle, start with the little you have, then stand back and watch what the Lord will do.

> *START WITH THE LITTLE YOU HAVE, THEN STAND BACK AND WATCH WHAT THE LORD WILL DO.*

GOD NEVER FORGETS

I've often wondered, "What happened to the twelve baskets that were left over?"

The Bible does not specifically say, but I have a good idea. Jesus once proclaimed: *"Give, and it will be given to you. A good measure, pressed down, shaken together and running over, will be poured into your lap. For with the measure you use, it will be measured to you"* (Luke 6:38).

This scripture gives me reason to believe the unlikely hero who gave Jesus five loaves and two fishes went home carrying twelve full baskets!

Man may not remember – or even know – the moments you have seized through faith, yet God

DO WHAT YOU CAN, WITH WHAT YOU HAVE, WHERE YOU ARE.

– THEODORE ROOSEVELT

never forgets. He will return everything you have given – plus so much more.

THEY'RE KNOWN TO GOD!

Even though you may be living in the shadows, God is watching. After talking about Noah, Abraham, Jacob, Joseph, Moses and Gideon, the writer of Hebrews presents the anonymous heroes of faith – the ones who *"were tortured and refused to be released, so that they might gain a better resurrection. Some faced jeers and flogging, while still others were chained and put in prison.*

> **EVEN THOUGH YOU MAY BE LIVING IN THE SHADOWS, GOD IS WATCHING.**

They were stoned; they were sawed in two; they were put to death by the sword. They went about in sheepskins and goatskins, destitute, persecuted and mistreated" (Hebrews 11:35-37).

These unknowns will also reap a bountiful reward.

LITTLE IS MUCH

As I shared in Step 1, when we began *Full Turn Youth Ministries*, all I had to offer the Lord was myself and a handful of teens. In the Master's hands, it was all that was needed.

Think of it this way. Even though I am not a chef, I know there are certain ingredients you must put in a cake to make it rise.

It's the same with your dream. If you want to achieve, it is vital to include the right elements. One fact is certain: if you include the Lord in the mix, a positive outcome is assured.

You may feel totally inadequate, yet *little is much when God is in it!* As the prophet Zechariah asked, *"Who despises the day of small things?"* (Zechariah 4:10).

Are you ready to become one of the Lord's heroes? Start with what you have and allow Him to do the rest.

CATCH THE SPIRIT OF A HERO

I once heard Benson Idahosa, a noted spiritual leader from Africa say, "If you want to be successful, surround yourself with successful people."

What they possess somehow spills over on you – and enhances your life.

Ask yourself these questions. What makes a hero excel? How do they consistently exceed expectations?

Talk to leaders in business, sports, politics or entertainment and they will often tell you of role models they admired and looked up to – someone who inspired their career. Many will even *quote* their hero.

A STRONG FOUNDATION

In this book I make reference to my father and

YOU NEVER KNOW WHEN A MOMENT AND A FEW SINCERE WORDS CAN HAVE AN IMPACT ON A LIFE.

– ZIG ZIGLAR

grandfather because they had such a dramatic impact on my life. I was affected by the principles they instilled, and by their contagious spirit.

Like a chain reaction, when we build on the foundation of others, someone will eventually be able to stand on *our* shoulders.

It's sad and such a waste when we cast aside the elderly thinking they are too old to be useful. Think of the wealth of knowledge and life experience they possess!

> *LIKE A CHAIN REACTION, WHEN WE BUILD ON THE FOUNDATION OF OTHERS, SOMEONE WILL EVENTUALLY BE ABLE TO STAND ON OUR SHOULDERS.*

DAVID, THE WARRIOR!

Let me tell you about one of the great heroes of the Old Testament. His name is David – the youngest son of a shepherd named Jesse.

Many picture David as a young boy sitting in a field, watching his flock of sheep, playing a harp and singing psalms to the Lord – a man after God's own heart (1 Samuel 13:14).

Few remember David as a great captain and warrior. He was so lionized by the people they would sing of his exploits in the streets: *"Saul has slain his*

THERE IS A DIFFERENCE
BETWEEN IMITATING
A GOOD MAN AND
COUNTERFEITING HIM.

– BENJAMIN FRANKLIN

thousands, and David his tens of thousands" (1 Samuel 18:7)

As you can imagine, Saul became extremely jealous and plotted to have David killed. Here was a young man who had been lauded and applauded – and anointed by God to be the future king of Israel (1 Samuel 16:13). Now he was running for his life!

A CREW OF REJECTS

David was at the lowest point of his journey, hiding in the cave of Adullam. I can only wonder how rejected, frustrated, and alone he must have felt.

The Bible records that when the word spread of his whereabouts, *"All those who were in distress or in debt or discontented gathered around him, and he became their leader. About four hundred men were with him"* (1 Samuel 22:2).

> **IT'S AMAZING TO THINK OF THE MIRACLE WHICH OCCURRED IN THAT CAVE.**

What a scene! Here was the heralded warrior surrounded by hundreds of outcasts – a ragged crew of lowlifes and rejects.

It's amazing to think of the miracle which occurred in that cave. These scorned, disdained men chose

MAKE EVERY EFFORT
TO KEEP THE UNITY OF
THE SPIRIT THROUGH
THE BOND OF PEACE.

– EPHESIANS 4:10

David to be their captain. They not only caught his spirit; they found a purpose for their lives and a reason to live!

From that moment forward, this same group of misfits became one of the greatest fighting forces the world had ever known.

THE HEART OF A CHAMPION

How could these men who had never conquered anything, or known the sweet taste of victory, be suddenly changed? They were inspired by the heart of a champion.

They did not appoint some loser as their captain. A voice within them urged, "If we are going to be great, we must identify with greatness."

> *"IF WE ARE GOING TO BE GREAT, WE MUST IDENTIFY WITH GREATNESS."*

David's army was so loyal that all he had to do was whisper something he wanted and they would risk their lives to obtain it (2 Samuel 23:13-17).

AMAZING FEATS

Here are just a few of the men who linked their hearts with David's. One was his chief captain, Adino

WHEN SOMEONE DOES SOMETHING GOOD, APPLAUD! YOU WILL MAKE TWO PEOPLE HAPPY.

– SAMUEL GOLDWYN

– a fearless warrior who *"raised his spear against eight hundred men, whom he killed in one encounter"* (2 Samuel 23:8).

Next in rank was Eleazar. He stood with David in a fierce battle at a place called Pas Dammim. Even when the Israelites retreated, Eleazar *"stood his ground and struck down the Philistines till his hand grew tired and froze to the sword. The Lord brought about a great victory that day"* (2 Samuel 23:10).

Then there was Shammah who single-handed defeated an entire regiment of the enemy in a bean patch! (v.11). Or how about Benaiah, who killed two giants from Moab, and was also known for jumping into a pit with a lion when it was snowing. Despite the slippery conditions, he killed the animal just for sport! (v.20).

> **THESE WERE DAVID'S TOP MEN – THEY CAUGHT HIS SPIRIT AND BECAME GREAT THEMSELVES.**

These were David's top men – they caught his spirit and became great themselves.

DUPLICATED EXPLOITS

Do you remember the story of David killing a lion and a bear while defending his sheep, or taking down

Goliath with just a slingshot and five smooth stones?

Now we find those early exploits being duplicated by men who embraced the heart of their leader. They too became mighty men of valor – and were handsomely rewarded when David entered the palace and ascended to the throne.

I hope you are beginning to grasp what can happen when we capture the heart of those God has placed in our lives. It marks the beginning of great blessings, mighty victories and a new level of anointing.

STEP 5

JOIN FORCES!

From as early as I can remember, my dad was my hero and I wanted to be just like him.

As a young boy I watched him play football and score touchdowns. I thought it was neat to listen to his band perform and hear him sing – yes, my dad was a rock and roller! To me he was always the best at everything.

In 1982, when I was seven years old, my father became the Senior Pastor of Gospel Harvester Church in Atlanta, Georgia. I can still remember how he took the church to new levels by breaking down traditional barriers and boldly speaking the truth of God's Word.

About two years later the Lord spoke to him concerning moving the church to a new location. With practically zero money in the bank, he stepped out in faith.

I had always admired him for his ability in sports

THE SECRET OF WINNING
FOOTBALL GAMES IS WORKING
MORE AS A TEAM, LESS AS
INDIVIDUALS. I PLAY NOT MY 11
BEST, BUT MY BEST 11.

– KNUTE ROCKNE

and music; now I was seeing him in a brand new light – defying the odds and moving forward with boldness. I had deep respect for his strength and courage.

It seemed whatever my father set his mind to was always accomplished.

MORE THAN GENETICS!

As I grew older, I traveled with dad as he ministered and touched the lives of thousands. During those times I began talking with him concerning things that truly mattered – life and vision.

Before long a transformation began stirring within me. Somehow, my heart became joined with his in ministry – and the qualities I admired in him started to be demonstrated in my own life.

> *IT WAS MORE THAN GENETICS – IT WAS SPIRITUAL!*

It was more than genetics – it was spiritual!

Now, as I have matured in ministry, I see the same things occurring in the lives of young men and women who have linked their hearts with mine.

JOINED AT THE HEART

Throughout the Bible we see the power of unity –

ALAN MUSHEGAN, JR.

TWO ARE BETTER
THAN ONE, BECAUSE THEY
HAVE A GOOD RETURN FOR
THEIR WORK: IF ONE FALLS
DOWN, HIS FRIEND CAN
HELP HIM UP.

– ECCLESIASTES 4:9-10

and how the anointing flows from the head down (Psalm 133:1-3).

When God told Moses *"Come up to me on the mountain and stay here, and I will give you the tablets of stone, with the law and commands I have written for their instruction"* (Exodus 24:12), there was only one other person who could go with him and live – his assistant, Joshua. This was because the two were joined at the heart. Later, when God looked upon Joshua He saw in him the spirit of Moses (Joshua 1:5).

> *"AS SURELY AS THE LORD LIVES AND YOU LIVE, I WILL NOT LEAVE YOU."*
> *– 2 KINGS 2:4*

That same relationship developed between the prophet Elijah and a young man he found plowing in a field – Elisha. Their bond was so strong that before the prophet was taken to heaven in a whirlwind, Elisha declared, *"As surely as the Lord lives and as you live, I will not leave you"* (2 Kings 2:4).

Because of this extraordinary level of commitment Elisha received a double portion of Elijah's spirit – and became one of the noted prophets of the Old Testament.

THE POWER OF CONNECTING

The words *"two will become one"* (Matthew 19:5)

ALL YOUR STRENGTH IS IN UNION. ALL YOUR DANGER IS IN DISCORD.

— *HENRY WADSWORTH LONGFELLOW*

refer to more than marriage – it is the foundation of *any* covenant.

One of the prime examples of unity is how Christ has joined Himself to His church *"for we are members of his body"* (Ephesians 5:30) – of His flesh, of His bones.

Christ prayed that all believers *"may be one"* (John 17:21). Because of this divine union we are able to grow and prosper. Jesus declared, *"I am the vine; you are the branches. If a man remains in me and I in him, he will bear much fruit; apart from me you can do nothing"* (John 15:5).

> *JUST AS ELECTRIC POWER BEGINS TO SURGE WHEN A CORD IS PLUGGED INTO AN OUTLET, TRUE LIFE FLOWS THROUGH OUR HEAVENLY CONNECTION.*

What happens when a limb is torn from a tree? That branch loses its source of life and withers.

Just as electric power begins to surge when a cord is plugged into an outlet, true life flows through our heavenly connection.

FLYING HIGH!

The single most valuable lesson I have learned in

ministry is the necessity of surrounding yourself with the right people – those who are spiritually committed, supportive and will help propel you forward rather than hold you back.

Instead of searching for people to inspire, start looking for people who can inspire *you!*

You've heard the old adage, "Birds of a feather flock together." If that is true, what kind of bird are you? Make certain those with whom you associate are quality individuals who share your vision and want to fly in the same direction.

Ultimate champions link their lives with greatness.

STEP 6

DON'T LET YOUR PAST DETERMINE YOUR FUTURE

As a freshman in high school, I decided to join the wrestling team. It was tough getting ready for my first season, yet I was filled with determination.

It would be wonderful to tell you how I won every match that year. Unfortunately, that's not what happened. The moment I stepped onto the mat, fear would fall over me with such force I could feel it deep in the pit of my stomach. When the whistle blew, it seemed all my hard work and practice went down the drain – and I wound up flat on my back!

My excuse was I had lost so much weight to wrestle in the 125-pound division I had no strength left for the contest.

I LIKE THE DREAMS OF THE FUTURE BETTER THAN THE HISTORY OF THE PAST.

– THOMAS JEFFERSON

I lost every match I entered – not because I didn't know what to do, but because I had already defeated myself in my mind.

The truth was unavoidable: *I did not believe I could win*.

After a disastrous season I decided if I was going to wrestle my sophomore year, I needed a totally new outlook and strategy. Tired of losing, I spent the entire summer in preparation – morning, noon and night.

As a result of a weight-training program, I gained thirty pounds and was no longer the skinny freshman who was afraid of his opponents. Inside, I was brimming with confidence and could hardly wait for the contests to start.

> *INSIDE, I WAS BRIMMING WITH CONFIDENCE AND COULD HARDLY WAIT FOR THE CONTESTS TO START.*

That year I won the majority of my matches and lettered in the sport.

IT'S TODAY THAT COUNTS

Later, I realized it was not the weight lifting that made the difference between a winning and a losing season. It was my attitude that changed – and I

IT IS VERY DANGEROUS, IF NOT A FATAL HABIT, TO JUDGE OURSELVES TO BE SAFE BECAUSE OF SOMETHING WE DID TWENTY YEARS AGO.

– CHARLES H. SPURGEON

refused to let my past determine my future!

I can still remember the Sunday morning before church when my grandfather sat me down and dispensed some of his life-building wisdom. He told me: "Your past is gone and you can't get yesterday back. Your tomorrow has not yet come so why worry about the future. Concentrate on today. Be the best that you can be this day and you will never have to worry about tomorrow again."

That truth is an essential key to success.

RIGHT CHOICES

Friend, if you want to become a champion, learn to break the cycle of living that causes you to remain in defeat. This means you must abandon harmful habits and replace them with something better.

> *IF YOU WANT TO BECOME A CHAMPION, LEARN TO BREAK THE CYCLE OF LIVING THAT CAUSES YOU TO REMAIN IN DEFEAT.*

Psychologists tell us it takes approximately 25 days to form a habit – repeating an action over and over until it becomes an automatic behavior.

Don't try to do this on your own; ask for God's help. The apostle Paul tells us in Christ we are *"a new*

THEREFORE, IF ANYONE
IS IN CHRIST, HE IS A NEW
CREATION; THE OLD
HAS GONE, THE NEW
HAS COME!

– 2 CORINTHIANS 5:17

creation" (2 Corinthians 5:17). The negative habits you have formed over the years must be destroyed and exchanged for the power of a resurrected lifestyle.

Just as the decisions you made yesterday have shaped what you are today, the choices you make *now* will directly affect your tomorrow.

I would love to give you a guarantee that the future will be better than what you are leaving behind. I can't. The hope of your tomorrow lies in what you are doing *right now* – what you are thinking in your heart at this very moment. The Bible tells us as a man *"thinketh in his heart, so is he"* (Proverbs 23:7 KJV).

> *THE HOPE OF YOUR TOMORROW LIES IN WHAT YOU ARE DOING RIGHT NOW.*

OUR GREAT HERITAGE

As God's children we come from a long line of heroes and have a great spiritual heritage. An understanding of this divine lineage provides the fuel to propel us toward the promise of tomorrow.

Abraham is known as the father of our faith – the first great champion we find in the Bible.

Here was a man who wasn't afraid of venturing into new territory. He left everything he had ever

IF WE OPEN A QUARREL
BETWEEN THE PAST AND THE
PRESENT, WE SHALL FIND THAT
WE HAVE LOST THE FUTURE.

– WINSTON CHURCHILL

known – his country and his people – to become what he was always destined to be. God told him, *"You will be the father of many nations"* (Genesis 17:4).

TOO OLD?

If you have doubts and worry you are too old for a fresh start, think about Abraham. He had already lived 75 years when he began this new phase of his life.

What if he had been fearful of moving out of the land in which he was born and raised? What if he used the excuse of his age to hinder him from obeying God?

If you plan to excel you cannot allow your past to dictate your future.

THE PROMISE

God established with Abraham an *everlasting* covenant (Gen. 12:1-13) – meaning it has no end.

Of the many covenants found in God's Word, Abraham's pact with the Almighty is the only one that includes a promise of being *forever*.

Even more, by accepting Jesus as Lord and Savior, we become inheritors of everything God assured to Abraham and his children: *"If you belong to Christ, then you are Abraham's seed, and heirs according to the promise"* (Galatians 3:29).

That makes us partakers of the same covenant and, like Abraham, we have a promise for tomorrow.

The religious leaders of Jesus' time listened to Him teach in the temple, yet refused to follow Him, saying, "Abraham is our father."

How did the Lord respond? *"If you were Abraham's children...then you would do the things Abraham did"* (John 8:39).

Abraham not only saw a "far off" promise, he lived a life which brought blessing and earned him the title "Friend of God" (James 2:23).

NEW BOUNDARIES

I'm sure you were taught as a child, "Don't put off until tomorrow what you can do today." Those words shouldn't be taken lightly – they contain great power. What you are doing this moment can open the doors you need to walk through next week, next month or next year.

I heard someone say that insanity is repeating the same action over and over again expecting a different result. If you want to experience change, be willing to venture beyond your present boundaries.

Remember, your yesterday doesn't determine your tomorrow!

STEP 7

BELIEVE YOU'RE A CHAMPION!

To experience the lifestyle of a hero, you need the *faith* and *belief* of a hero. This means you may need to swim in uncharted waters.

What is faith? The Bible defines it as *"the confident assurance that something we want is going to happen. It is the certainty that what we hope for is waiting for us, even though we cannot see it up ahead"* (Hebrews. 11:1 TLB).

IS IT POSSIBLE?

In Step 6 we talked about the covenant God made with Abraham – and one of the promises was the Lord would give him a son. The Lord told him, *"a son coming from your own body will be your heir"* (Genesis 15:4).

FAITH IS LIKE RADAR
THAT SEES THROUGH THE FOG
– THE REALITY OF THINGS AT A
DISTANCE THAT THE HUMAN
EYE CANNOT SEE.

– CORRIE TEN BOOM

In the natural, Abraham had doubts. After all, he and his wife, Sarah, were getting on in years. Later, when God repeated the promise, *"Abraham fell facedown; he laughed and said to himself, 'Will a son be born to a man a hundred years old? Will Sarah bear a child at the age of ninety?'"* (Genesis 17:17).

Despite his questions, he still believed.

When Sarah smiled at the idea, God asked, *"Is anything too hard for the Lord?"* (Genesis 18:14).

NEVER STOP BELIEVING IN YOUR GOD-GIVEN VISION – REGARDLESS OF HOW IMPROBABLE IT MAY SEEM.

They trusted God and witnessed the birth of their son Isaac. The Bible says, *"By faith Abraham, even though he was past age – and Sarah herself was barren – was enabled to become a father because he considered him faithful who had made the promise"* (Hebrews 11:11).

Never stop believing in your God-given vision – regardless of how improbable it may seem. Remember the words of Jesus: *"With man this is impossible, but with God all things are possible"* (Matthew 19:26).

THE SEED

One of the greatest lies a person can buy into is

BELIEVE THAT YOU WILL SUCCEED. BELIEVE IT FIRMLY, AND THEN YOU WILL DO WHAT IS NECESSARY TO BRING ABOUT SUCCESS.

– DALE CARNEGIE

this: "You have nothing to offer. Zero!"

Everyone – regardless of their background or upbringing, has something of value to bring to the table of life.

Before you were ever born, a seed of greatness was placed within you. What you must discover is how to nurture that seed.

> *BEFORE YOU WERE EVER BORN, A SEED OF GREATNESS WAS PLACED WITHIN YOU.*

I'm not saying you were *born* a champion: rather, you were born with the inherent ability you need to *become* one by putting God's principles into practice.

OVERCOMING THE ODDS

I thank the Lord every day for the wonderful legacy He has given me. My family tree is filled with men and women who have accomplished marvelous things for the kingdom of God. However, none of these people reached their potential overnight.

Let me tell you about one of these heroes – a man who, with God's help, overcame the odds and became a champion. He is my great-grandfather, Earl P. Paulk, Sr. For many years he was a distinguished leader in the Church of God, serving as the Assistant

NOW FAITH IS BEING SURE OF WHAT WE HOPE FOR AND CERTAIN OF WHAT WE DO NOT SEE.

– HEBREWS 1:11

General Overseer for the denomination and one of the first ministers to broadcast church services on radio.

During his tenure in Greenville, South Carolina, the church grew to become one of the largest and most successful in the United States.

"The Walking Bible"

His life, however, wasn't always a mountain-top experience. My great-grandfather was born on a small farm in South Georgia – and like many children of his day, he quit school to help take care of the daily chores. He dropped out in the third grade.

> *He Would Memorize the Verses She Read and Soon was Able to Recite them by Heart.*

After a personal encounter with the Holy Spirit at the age of 17, he began preaching. My grandmother, Myrtle Mushegan (his eldest daughter), once told me that early in his ministry he would have his young wife, – whom he affectionately called Addie Mae – read the Bible to him because he wasn't able to read.

He would memorize the verses she read and soon

THE ONLY THING THAT
STANDS BETWEEN A MAN AND
WHAT HE WANTS FROM LIFE IS
OFTEN MERELY THE WILL TO
TRY IT AND THE FAITH TO
BELIEVE IT IS POSSIBLE.

– RICHARD M. DEVOS

was able to recite them by heart. He quickly became known as "The Walking Bible" for his ability to quote hundreds of scriptures accurately during his messages. Later in life he learned to read by sounding out the words of the verses he had already memorized.

A ROYAL WELCOME

Here was a man who once struggled with illiteracy, yet eventually sat on the board of two outstanding colleges. He became such a great community leader he was invited to have tea in the Bahamas with King Edward VIII, the former King of England. On another occasion he joined John F. Kennedy at the White House for a breakfast. They were curious about his success.

> *HE BELIEVED IN HIMSELF AND THE GIFT GOD HAD PLACED WITHIN HIM – AND NEVER SAW HIS BACKGROUND AS A BARRIER.*

What was his secret? He believed in himself and the gift God had placed within him – and never saw his background as a barrier. Because of his faith, failure was not an option.

YOUR REWARD

What you hope for is much closer than you realize

if you will dare to believe. That is how we access the provisions of God. Scripture declares that *"without faith it is impossible to please God, because anyone who comes to him must believe that he exists and that he rewards those who earnestly seek him"* (Hebrews 11:6).

Just because you can't see the prize does not mean it doesn't exist. When the Lord makes a promise, He keeps it.

Hope against hope. Believe beyond belief. Stand on the assurance that *all* things are possible!

GET TOUGH ON YOURSELF!

The title "hero," doesn't come easily. Believe me, there is always a steep price to pay.

Let me tell you about my great-grandfather on my dad's side, Aram Mushegan. He died when I was just three years old, yet he left an imprint on my life.

Aram was born in Armenia and was forced to leave his country because certain Turkish people were slaughtering Armenians because of their faith in Jesus Christ. At the word of an old Russian prophet, he and his family left everything behind and sailed for America on a cattle boat.

"You have to keep on keeping on" was the motto of his life – and a phrase that is still echoed in our family. Every time I face a difficult situation, I remember those words of my great-grandfather.

DESTINY IS NOT A MATTER
OF CHANCE, IT IS A MATTER
OF CHOICE; IT IS NOT A THING
TO BE WAITED FOR, IT IS A
THING TO BE ACHIEVED.

– WILLIAM JENNINGS BRYAN

A VOICE ON THE WATER

Aram's son, Harry (my grandfather) was born into this immigrant family in Los Angeles. He became a hard-working teenager, including holding down a job at a steel company.

One day, while out swimming in the Pacific Ocean, Harry listened as the unmistakable voice of the Lord called out to him. Several times he heard these words: "Where will you spend eternity?"

On that sandy beach he fell to his knees and asked Jesus to come into his heart and forgive his sin – and he has been a faithful servant of the Lord from that moment forward.

HE HEARD THESE WORDS: "WHERE WILL YOU SPEND ETERNITY?"

His ministry began on the street corners of Los Angeles where he played his guitar and preached. Saving every penny from his work, he eventually had enough to buy a gospel tent – and blazed a trail across America proclaiming the Word of the Lord.

THE DREAM LIVES ON

As a direct result of his obedience to God's call, prominent churches were built and many outstanding

GIVE ME A STOCK CLERK
WHO WANTS TO WORK AND
I WILL GIVE YOU A PERSON WHO
WILL MAKE HISTORY. GIVE ME
A PERSON WHO DOES NOT
WANT TO WORK, AND I WILL
GIVE YOU A STOCK CLERK.

– J. C. PENNEY

Christian leaders were brought into the Kingdom. Bishop Harry A. Mushegan's life touched hundreds of thousands of people – those who knew him and many who didn't.

He listened to a voice that was more powerful than the waves crashing on the beach – and his entire future was forever changed. Because he was faithful in the tough, difficult times, he can now sit back and see his dream live on through the lives of his children, his grandchildren, and the multitudes he influenced.

WHERE WILL YOU START?

It doesn't matter *where* you begin, but *that* you begin! Stop waiting for others to facilitate your dream and start living it. Good things come to those who are prepared to work, sweat and labor.

IT'S ONLY WHEN YOU PUT A WHEEL INTO MOTION THAT IT PICKS UP SPEED.

You have to start somewhere. Present what you have to the Lord and watch as He multiplies it in His hands.

It's only when you put a wheel into motion that it picks up speed. In our own ministry I call it the "snowball effect." When we started the ball rolling

WHATEVER YOUR HAND FINDS
TO DO, DO IT WITH ALL YOUR
MIGHT, FOR IN THE GRAVE...
THERE IS NEITHER WORKING NOR
PLANNING NOR KNOWLEDGE
NOR WISDOM.

– ECCLESIASTES 9:10

downhill it grew – and continued to grow.

My friend, you must make the first move before God supplies the miracle. The Bible says, *"Draw nigh to God, and he will draw nigh to you"* (James 4:8 KJV).

BE WILLING TO TRY

At times we are our own worst enemy. The battle we face is an inner-conflict between our mind and our spirit – and it often results in fear.

> **THE BATTLE WE FACE IS AN INNER-CONFLICT BETWEEN OUR MIND AND OUR SPIRIT – AND IT OFTEN RESULTS IN FEAR.**

Your spirit may be driving you forward, yet your mind is taunting you, "Don't do it! You may fail – you may even get hurt!"

As a child, when I was afraid to attempt something new, those around me would say, "You will never know unless you try!"

I still heed those words.

DEALING WITH CHANGE

Becoming a champion means there is a transformation taking place inside you, and it's often difficult for our carnal thoughts to deal with.

73

Paul tells us our mind is the enemy of God: *"Those who live according to the sinful nature have their minds set on what that nature desires; but those who live in accordance with the Spirit have their minds set on what the Spirit desires. The mind of sinful man is death, but the mind controlled by the Spirit is life and peace"* (Romans 8:5-6).

On what side of the ledger are your thoughts?

THE BATTLE INSIDE

To defeat the enemy of faith you must not only be committed to change, but passionate about finding the winner within – and this will take all the self-discipline you can muster. In other words, you need to get tough on yourself!

Make a list of the actions necessary to benefit you physically, emotionally, financially and spiritually. Next, put these things into practice.

If your daily routine is not making a positive contribution to your life, why are you wasting your time?

Please understand when I say "emotionally" I am not referring to something that will bring temporal pleasure. Rather, it concerns your emotional well being.

DO THE MATH!

Here's an equation that will help you overcome your fears and allow you to walk in faith:

Discipline + Desire = Achieving your dream.

When we talk about turning vision into reality, this equation becomes necessary.

Start by targeting the aspects of your life that need improvement – your areas of greatest weakness:

- Do you have a negative attitude?
- Are you unhappy with your physical condition?
- Do you have a problem with insecurity?
- Are you depressed over your financial situation?
- Do you feel spiritually healthy?

IT'S YOUR TURN!

When you determine what the problem is, ask yourself, "What am I going to do to correct it?"

For example, bodybuilders concentrate on different muscle groups every day. That's how they are able to maximize their workout and get the results they desire.

EVEN IF YOU'RE ON THE RIGHT TRACK, YOU'LL GET RUN OVER IF YOU JUST SIT THERE.

– WILL ROGERS

They focus more time and energy on areas of weakness, rather than their strength.

Why? Because they know what they want to *become*. As the Bible tells us: *"Faith without works is dead"* (James 2:17 KJV).

You'll only find the right level of discipline when you clearly understand what you want to achieve.

FIRE IN YOUR BONES!

Next comes desire and tenacity. Do you have the passion necessary to hold onto your dream? The prophet Jeremiah called it *"a burning fire shut up in my bones"* (Jeremiah 20:9).

When a deep expectation is added to a disciplined lifestyle, you have found the key that unlocks your full potential.

> **WHEN A DEEP EXPECTATION IS ADDED TO A DISCIPLINED LIFESTYLE, YOU HAVE FOUND THE KEY THAT UNLOCKS YOUR FULL POTENTIAL.**

"CARPE DIEM!"

A true hero is always looking for another winning moment, another obstacle to overcome, another chance at greatness – one more moment in time that will make the difference. Sure, a conqueror bears many scars, however, each serves as a reminder of a battle that has been fought and won.

Life is made up of the moments we capture or those we allow to slip though our fingers. Now is the time to "carpe diem" – seize the day!

Stop making excuses for coming in second best. The apostle Paul asks: *"Do you not know that in a race all the runners run, but only one gets the prize? Run in such a way as to get the prize"* (1 Corinthians 9:24).

Only those who are committed, passionate and focused will complete the journey.

Don't give up when victory is within your grasp. Just "keep on keeping on!"

STEP 9

DON'T LISTEN TO THE CROWD

Y ou've probably concluded that I love to watch professional boxing and amateur wrestling. One thing I have learned by observing these sports is that a good fighter will always stay focused. Their adversary may mock them and people may be chanting their opponent's name, yet regardless of what is happening around them, they stay fixed on their target.

If you plan to be victorious, your ultimate goal must become an obsession.

In a boxing ring, a fighter's strategy is to position the opponent in such a way that it's possible for a knockout blow – always looking for an opening. The slightest hesitation can cause that plan to fail.

My father once told me: "In your distraction is your destruction." How true.

One glance at the crowd, one second of letting

IT'S WHAT YOU DO ON THE
FIELD THAT COUNTS, NOT WHAT
YOU SAY. YOU CAN WIN THE
BATTLE OF THE PRESS, PLEASE
ALL YOUR CRITICS AND
STILL LOSE THE GAME.

– CHUCK NOLL

your guard down, and POW! That's why it is imperative to keep your eye on the goal.

They Laughed!

When I began working in youth ministry at the age of sixteen, there were voices coming at me from every side – including words of criticism.

- "How can someone so young be able to run a youth ministry?"
- "There's no way he can effectively do the job."

In the beginning it seemed whatever I attempted was ridiculed. I even overheard one of my closest friends – a man who was supposed to be helping me – laughing at my efforts. I was crushed!

I worried, "What will people think if I try that?"

Soon I was so confused and discouraged that it seemed all the enthusiasm and energy I once had was being drained from me. Instead of implementing new ideas, I worried, "What will people think if I try that?"

Here was the problem: I stopped listening to the

GOD HIMSELF, SIR, DOES NOT PROPOSE TO JUDGE A MAN UNTIL HIS LIFE IS OVER. WHY SHOULD YOU AND I?

– SAMUEL JOHNSON

heavenly voice that had led me to a place of leadership and started reacting to those around me.

THEY'RE FICKLE!

Let me put it bluntly. There is no way to run with the crowd and become a hero. They may love you one minute and the next they are out to annihilate you. The crowd is fickle!

> *THERE IS NO WAY TO RUN WITH THE CROWD AND BECOME A HERO.*

What a great moment of freedom when I finally realized this truth.

Today, the ministry so many criticized has become one of the largest and most effective youth outreaches in the nation. In addition to the hundreds of teens whose lives are being touched at our *Full Turn* meetings – we reach out to a potential audience of millions through our weekly television program.

ONLY ONE VOICE

Here's what is so amazing. The very things people denounced in the beginning have become the keys to our success today.

Have the negative voices stopped? Not all of them. I have learned that everyone has an opinion, but if you

FOR WHAT DO RIGHTEOUSNESS AND WICKEDNESS HAVE IN COMMON? OR WHAT FELLOWSHIP CAN LIGHT HAVE WITH DARKNESS?

– 2 CORINTHIANS 6:14

are going to succeed you must stay true to your calling and vision. Certainly, I am aware of what people say, yet there is only one voice that matters – the sound of the Master, speaking directly to my heart.

Remember, you were not placed on earth to serve the diverse opinions of man. You are here to fulfill your divine purpose – and the only one you need to be concerned about serving is God. It is His voice you must obey.

"Son, Just Relax!"

Another valuable lesson my father taught me is to tune out the world and stay focused and relaxed. Whether it was playing baseball, karate, wrestling, singing, studying or working in the church, his advice always remained the same.

> *"Relax and Keep Doing What You Know to Do. Don't Worry About Anybody Else's Opinion."*

I can still remember when I was frustrated with my performance in sports – or confused with how things were going in my life. Dad's response didn't change: "Son, relax and keep doing what you know to do. Don't worry about anybody else's opinion. Just keep your eye on the vision and everything is going to be alright."

Today, when I am speaking at a conference, playing a concert with our Christian band, or making everyday decisions, his words keep ringing in my ears: "Son, just relax!"

DON'T LOOK BACK!

In this fight of faith, the enemy would like nothing better than to distract you long enough to see you fall on your back wondering "What on earth happened?" That's why you must relax and rest in Him – keeping focused on the goal God has inspired you to accomplish.

Say these words aloud: "God's vision for my life is my obsession. My dream is my passion!"

If you believe what you have just said, don't look back – the moment you give an opening to the enemy he will take full advantage.

Instead, listen to the inner voice of the Master. It's only His direction that matters.

STICK TO THE PLAN

Earlier in this book, I shared my first passion in life – the desire to become a karate champion. At the age of 12, after absorbing myself in the sport for several years I reached my goal – a junior black belt.

At that moment something inside of me changed. My desire to keep advancing was over. I stopped attending classes, discontinued reading martial arts magazines and quit watching kung fu movies.

As I look back, my dream ended because I had reached my ultimate objective. In my young mind, there was nothing else to strive for.

ONLY A STEPPING STONE

A milestone should never become your final

IF A MAN HASN'T DISCOVERED SOMETHING HE WILL DIE FOR, HE ISN'T FIT TO LIVE.

— MARTIN LUTHER KING, JR.

destination; it's just a stepping stone on your journey. After achieving one goal, you must aim for the next level – and the next, then the next.

Don't give up or settle for less. Remember, you only achieve what your desire demands – and you can only rise as high as you allow yourself to.

> *YOU ONLY ACHIEVE WHAT YOUR DESIRE DEMANDS – AND YOU CAN ONLY RISE AS HIGH AS YOU ALLOW YOURSELF TO.*

BE PATIENT

Let's be honest. Having patience isn't easy.

I'm sure someone has told you, "All good things come in time." As much as we hate to admit it, that statement is true.

We read the stories of Bible heroes and exclaim, "Wow! I wish that would happen for me!"

Yet, what we fail to recognize is that patience is required to achieve greatness. Jesus said, *"In your patience possess ye your souls"* (Luke21: 19 KJV).

In the Genesis account we learn that man was created spirit, soul, and body. God breathed into Adam the breath of life and he became *"a living soul"* (Genesis 2:7).

The soul part of you is your personality – it is who

NO ONE WOULD EVER HAVE CROSSED THE OCEAN IF HE COULD HAVE GOTTEN OFF THE SHIP IN A STORM.

– CHARLES F. KETTERING

and what you are.

Only by patiently "walking out" what God has said will you discover your true self and what you are capable of achieving.

James, the brother of Jesus observed: *"For when your patience is in full bloom, then you will be ready for anything, strong in character, full and complete"* (James 1:2 TLB).

If you truly want to find your potential, learn the art of patience. In the process you'll experience personal growth and development.

IT'S A PROCESS

Let me assure you the Almighty will never ask you to do something you cannot handle. The Lord knows you better than you know yourself – including what your abilities are. Remember, He gave them to you!

> *THE ALMIGHTY WILL NEVER ASK YOU TO DO SOMETHING YOU CANNOT HANDLE.*

God wants to see if you are willing to grow into what He has destined you to become.

When I was a child I desperately wanted to be an adult – with all its advantages. However, I learned there was a process of maturing that had to take place before that could occur.

The same applies to growing in grace. Through patience we take hold of the promises of God and we are able to walk into our calling – full and complete."

DIVINE ORDERS

The Father's plan for your future requires both patience and obedience.

It's been said: "You cannot teach an old dog new tricks." I disagree with this statement. When men and women learn the law of being obedient they are able to accomplish just about anything.

The power that we have in Christ derives from our willingness to serve Him and to follow His divine orders. Jesus said, *"If you love me, you will obey what I command"* (John 14:15).

ON MOUNT MORIAH

Earlier, we talked about the patience exhibited by Abraham while he waited for the promise. There was also a time when his obedience was put to the test.

God asked Abraham to sacrifice his only son as a burnt offering. The next morning, without argument, he took Isaac to mount Moriah and built a sacrificial altar – even tying his son down on the wood and raising his knife.

This is the same son that Abraham waited so long for – and whom he loved dearly. You may question, "How could he do such a thing?"

YOUR PROVIDER

Remember, before Isaac was born God signed an everlasting covenant with Abraham *"and your descendants after you for the generations to come"* (Genesis 17:7).

This is why Abraham was able to face such a difficult task and remain faithful to the voice of the Lord. When Isaac asked him, "Where is the lamb for the burnt offering?" Abraham answered, *"God himself will provide"* (Genesis 22:8).

> *"GOD HIMSELF WILL PROVIDE."*
> *– GENESIS 22:8*

Suddenly, Abraham heard a voice from heaven saying, *"Do not lay a hand on the boy...Do not do anything to him. Now I know that you fear God, because you have not withheld from me your son, your only son"* (v.12).

BETTER THAN SACRIFICE

The Lord had never failed Abraham, and he knew

IF YOU AREN'T GOING ALL THE WAY, WHY GO AT ALL?

– JOE NAMATH

this test would be no different. If God said His covenant included Isaac, there was no way his son would die. The Word says that *"to obey is better than sacrifice"* (1 Samuel 15:22).

Because of Abraham's obedience, the Lord declared, *"I will surely bless you and make your descendants as numerous as the stars in the sky and as the sand on the seashore"* (v.17).

> **WHEN YOU UNDERSTAND THE PROMISES GOD HAS GIVEN YOU...IT IS EASY TO LIVE AN OBEDIENT LIFESTYLE.**

When you understand the promises God has given you – and that He honors His Word above His own name – it is easy to live an obedient lifestyle.

HEED THE INSTRUCTIONS

I once heard of a man who hired a carpenter to build a house. He presented the plan and gave the builder all the specifications necessary to complete the project, including the exact location where it was to be built. Then the owner left on a trip.

When he returned, the house was finished – except for one problem. The carpenter built it on the other side of the street, saying, "I thought it was a much better location."

As you can imagine, the owner was furious. "I'm not paying you a dime. You built a great house, but that's not where I asked you to construct it."

Many are like that with God. They feel they are following His plan because they are involved in doing good works. The question is: are they following the Lord's specific instructions?

Walking in blessing means we are in total obedience to God.

THE WAY OF EXCELLENCE

Do you recall the story of Cain and Abel? One of the brothers, Abel, gave "a more excellent sacrifice" because it was given in obedience. Both men presented an offering, yet only what was given according to God's command was accepted (Genesis 4:3-5).

If you want to receive God's promise, stick to the plan. Since the Lord honors His Word, you should too.

GIVE LIKE A CHAMPION!

O ne of the great days in my life was when I realized the power of the principle I am about to share. It's what I call the "covenant connector."

If you desire to take on the true nature of a champion, learn how to be a giver.

God blessed Abraham because he was a tither (Genesis 14:17-20). That means he presented the Lord with a tenth of everything he received.

You may ask, "What does giving have to do with achieving?" When you read God's Word you understand the vital link.

A "HUNDREDFOLD" RETURN

Here was the situation Abraham faced. When he

WE MAKE A LIVING
BY WHAT WE GET.
WE MAKE A LIFE
BY WHAT WE GIVE.

– *WINSTON CHURCHILL*

heard that his nephew, Lot, had been taken captive and robbed of his possessions, he took 318 of his servants, formed an army and routed the enemy (Genesis 14:14-15).

Abraham not only rescued Lot, but brought back a bounty of goods (v.16).

Immediately, he met with the high priest, Melchizedek, and received God's blessing. When the spiritual leader reminded Abraham that it was the Lord who had given him the victory, Abraham honored the Lord with *"a tenth of everything"* (v.20).

Later in the book of Genesis we find his son, Isaac, sowing seed in a time of famine – and *"reaped a hundredfold, because the Lord blessed him"* (Genesis 26:12). Isaac's son, Jacob, also presented his tithe to the Lord. He said, *"of all that you give me I will give you a tenth"* (Genesis 28:22).

> *HE "REAPED A HUNDREDFOLD, BECAUSE THE LORD BLESSED HIM."*
> *– GENESIS 26:12*

Abraham understood the importance of being connected to the promises of God through the tithe – and taught this great principle of blessing to his children.

GIVE, AND IT SHALL BE
GIVEN UNTO YOU; GOOD
MEASURE, PRESSED DOWN,
AND SHAKEN TOGETHER,
AND RUNNING OVER.

– LUKE 6:38

Pass it On!

Hundreds of years later, Moses instructed the children of Israel concerning the covenant of tithing. Speaking on behalf of the Almighty, he said: *"All the tithe of the land, whether of the seed of the land, or of the fruit of the tree, is the Lord's: it is holy unto the Lord"* (Leviticus 27:30).

In the book of Malachi, the Almighty asks: *"Will a man rob God? Yet you rob me. But you ask, 'How do we rob you?' In tithes and offerings"* (Malachi 3:8).

It's for Today!

What did Jesus say about tithing? He called the Pharisees hypocrites, declaring, *"You give a tenth*

> *"All of the Tithe...is Holy Unto the Lord."*
> *– Leviticus 27:30*

of your spices – mint, dill and cummin. But you have neglected the more important matters of the law – justice, mercy and faithfulness. You should have practiced the latter, without neglecting the former" (Matthew 23:23). In other words, tithing is for today.

Where do you present your tithe? Abraham presented it to God's representative – Melchizedek.

Today, we bring what belongs to the Lord to the church to which we are joined. The Bible says *"'Bring* the whole tithe into the storehouse, that there may be food in my house. Test me in this,' says the Lord Almighty, 'and see if I will not throw open the floodgates of heaven and pour out so much blessing that you will not have room enough for it'" (Malachi 3:10).

THE BLESSING CONTINUES

The pact God made with Abraham is still valid: "And you are heirs of the prophets and of the covenant God made with your fathers. He said to Abraham, 'Through your offspring all peoples on earth will be blessed'" (Acts 3:25).

The connection between tithing and receiving a covenant blessing is undeniable. That's why true champions are not takers, they are givers!

TAP INTO YOUR HIDDEN POWER

What an incredible age! With the click of a mouse our email is received in Europe, and at the speed of light we can send a photo to a friend in Fiji.

Leading technology firms are constantly searching for new, ingenious ways we can interact with one another, but I believe the earthly forms of communication are equivalent to the "tin can and string" theory compared to our direct line to God through prayer.

When we fellowship with the Father, we suddenly tap into a source of hidden power beyond our human comprehension. It's how the Lord reveals His purpose for our life.

It was only by keeping the line to heaven open that God gave me the vision for the ministry in which we

THE THEME OF OUR GENERATION IS "GET MORE, KNOW MORE, AND DO MORE," INSTEAD OF "PRAY MORE, BE MORE, AND SERVE MORE."

– BILLY GRAHAM

are now involved. I owe *everything* to the time I spend talking with the Father and meditating on His Word.

Success comes through the Holy Spirit – our constant connection to the Father. That is what gives us access to God.

A HEAVENLY RELATIONSHIP

Earlier, we talked about God's promise to Abraham – a man who understood the power of having an intimate relationship with the Lord. At the beginning of his spiritual adventure, he went to a place near Bethel: *"There he built an altar to the Lord and called on the name of the Lord"* (Genesis 12:8).

> *"THERE HE BUILT AN ALTAR...AND CALLED ON THE NAME OF THE LORD."*
> – GENESIS 12:8

The Almighty had spoken to others before him, but Abraham not only listened, he took time to have fellowship with God. In those encounters, the Lord would unveil more and more of the plan for his future. It was Abraham's intercession for the sinful city of Sodom that saved Lot and his family (Genesis 18:16-33).

You can have the same personal relationship with your Heavenly Father by taking the time to commune daily with Him.

WHY NOT ASK?

Millions live powerless lives because they refuse to ask the Creator of all things for His wisdom and insight. Talk to the One who knows the end from the beginning – the One who gave you life. Let Him show you, step-by-step, what you need to accomplish, and *how!*

God's Word declares, *"Ye have not, because ye ask not"* (James 4:2).

If you want a surge of energy that will elevate you to new heights, plug into your hidden source of power.

STEP 13

BECOME A SERVANT

O ne day the mother of James and John – whom Jesus called the *"Sons of Thunder"* (Mark 3:17) – asked the Lord for a favor. It was just before the trial and crucifixion of Christ. Kneeling before Jesus with her sons, she requested, *"Grant that one of these two sons of mine may sit at your right and the other at your left in your kingdom"* (Matthew 20:21).

Jesus wasn't sure they knew what they were asking. He replied, *"Can you drink the cup I am going to drink?"* (V.22).

"We can," they answered.

The Lord continued, *"You will indeed drink from my cup, but to sit at my right or left is not for me to grant. These places belong to those for whom they have been prepared by my Father"* (Matthew 20:23).

DO ALL THE GOOD YOU CAN,
BY ALL THE MEANS YOU CAN,
IN ALL THE WAYS YOU CAN,
IN ALL THE PLACES YOU CAN,
AT ALL THE TIMES YOU CAN,
TO ALL THE PEOPLE YOU CAN,
AS LONG AS YOU EVER CAN.

– JOHN WESLEY

FOLLOWING COMES FIRST

When the ten other disciples heard about this request, they were indignant with the two brothers.

Jesus called them together and said, *"You know that the rulers of the Gentiles lord it over them, and their high officials exercise authority over them. Not so with you. Instead, whoever wants to become great among you must be your servant, and whoever wants to be first must be your slave – just as the Son of Man did not come to be served, but to serve, and to give his life as a ransom for many"* (Matthew 20:25-28).

> **IF YOU PLAN TO BE A LEADER, YOU MUST LEARN HOW TO FOLLOW.**

In this passage Jesus gives us the key to greatness: If you plan to be a leader, you must learn how to follow. The principle applies not only in God's Kingdom, but also in our work here on earth.

READY TO RESPOND

The apostle Paul wrote to the believers at Thessalonica, *"But let us, who are of the day, be sober, putting on the breastplate of faith and love; and for an helmet, the hope of salvation"* (1 Thessalonians 5:8).

To be *sober* means you are awake and alert –

IF I LOVE JESUS CHRIST, I WILL SERVE HUMANITY, THOUGH MEN AND WOMEN TREAT ME AS A DOORMAT.

– OSWALD CHAMBERS

ready to respond.

When you visit a restaurant with outstanding service, a good waitperson will always be aware of your needs before you have to ask. If your glass needs a refill, they are standing by with a pitcher. That's their job – to watch your table with diligence, anticipating your every wish.

What about you? Are you aware of your calling to such a degree that you are waiting for an opportunity to answer before someone asks?

The work of God on earth is fulfilled by those who are watchful. That's how the needs of His ministry are met.

SERVING TOGETHER

You begin the process of serving the Lord by aligning yourself to a church with a vision that is ordained by God. When you find that special place of worship, offer yourself to be used by the leadership – in whatever capacity they request.

THE LORD HAS A SPECIFIC WORK FOR EACH OF US, YET HE DESIRES THAT WE FLOW AS ONE IN SERVICE.

The Lord has a specific work for each of us, yet He desires that we flow as one in service. As David wrote: *"Behold, how good and how pleasant it is for brethren* to dwell together in unity!" (Psalm 133:1 KJV).

In the heart of David was the secret that made him a revered king – and produced powerful people who followed him.

Since this principle is universal, ask yourself, "What is my dream?"

Do you desire a successful business? Do you want to excel in the arts? Are you called to the mission field? Start by serving and you will be surprised what God will do!

LEARN FROM THE MASTER TEACHER

Like a phoenix, true heroes will often arise out of the ashes. The Lord will miraculously take the things we least expect and use them to transform lives.

Here's how Paul explains it: *"God chose the foolish things of the world to shame the wise; God chose the weak things of the world to shame the strong. He chose the lowly things of this world and the despised things – and the things that are not – to nullify the things that are"* (1 Corinthians 1:27-28).

The gifts and calling of the Lord will remain buried until you receive the life of the Father through the quickening power of the Holy Spirit. That's how the Lord allows what He has planted in your heart to grow and manifest itself.

When you place yourself totally in the hands of the Lord, He will transform your weakness into strength,

WHAT GOD DOES NOT CHOOSE TO GIVE, YOU CANNOT TAKE.

– JEWISH PROBERB

and your abilities into true power.

I have always loved hearing stories and watching films about men and women who defy incredible odds and overcome their obstacles. One of the most memorable motion pictures ever produced was *The Ten Commandments* – the story of Moses. It was captured on the big screen by Cecil B. DeMille.

> *HE WILL TRANSFORM YOUR WEAKNESS INTO STRENGTH, AND YOUR ABILITIES INTO TRUE POWER.*

OUT OF THE BULRUSHES

When Moses was just an infant, the king of Egypt, Pharaoh, issued a decree that every male child born to Hebrew slaves was to be killed.

The mother of Moses placed him in a tiny ark made of bulrushes and hid him in the reeds of the river near the banks of the Nile. He was found by Pharaoh's daughter who had compassion and took him to the palace where he was raised as the grandson of the king.

As he grew older, Moses was dismayed at the terrible persecution of his people and killed an Egyptian who was beating one of his Hebrew brothers.

IT IS GOD WHO ARMS ME WITH STRENGTH AND MAKES MY WAY PERFECT.

– PSALM 18:32

When Pharaoh heard about the incident he became angry and sought to take the life of Moses.

Immediately, he fled from Egypt and wound up in a place called Midian – where he married the daughter of a man named Jethro.

THE DELIVERER!

One afternoon, while Moses was out watching Jethro's sheep, an angel of the Lord appeared to him as a flaming bush and gave him the message that he was to deliver his people out of the clutches of Pharaoh.

Moses returned to Egypt where God showed Himself strong on Moses' behalf. Finally, after a series of plagues upon Pharaoh and his people, the king reluctantly released the children of Israel.

FROM PRACTICALLY NOTHING, GOD RAISED UP A DELIVERER FOR HIS PEOPLE.

The message of this dramatic story is that from practically *nothing*, God raised up a *deliverer* for His people. Moses went from a slave to a prince, then to a man running for his life. He was watching sheep on the backside of the desert when the Almighty brought him back to Egypt to become a hero for all times.

HOLD ON!

My friend, everything you are going through is shaping you into what the Lord is planning for your future.

I can tell you from experience that life often resembles a roller coaster ride, but hold on! Cling to the promises of God and He will teach you everything necessary to be a champion.

The psalmist wrote, *"Except the Lord build the house, they labor in vain that build it"* (Psalm 127:1 KJV). The original text means unless God instructs or trains His people, nothing will result from what they are trying to accomplish.

Enroll in the classes of the Master Teacher. He will give you the divine education you need.

STEP 15

BREAK THE BARRIERS!

If you were to ask me, "Who is the greatest champion who ever lived?" I would tell you about the one person who deserves such a distinction.

This Hero walked on water, spoke to storms, turned water into wine, raised people from the dead, turned five loaves of bread and two fishes into enough food to feed thousands, and still had time to conquer death hell and the grave!

You know of whom I speak – the Ultimate Champion, Jesus Christ.

When you read of His feats, they seem unbelievable, however, all of the miracles recorded in Scripture truly happened. They were written and testified to by many witnesses.

The People Who Get On in this World are Those Who Look for Circumstances they Want, and, If They Can't Find Them, Make Them.

– George Bernard Shaw

New Thoughts

Perhaps you have heard the song, "To Be Like Jesus. " Those are wonderful words, yet if you want to become like this Hero you must learn to *think* like Him.

The thought process of the Master is quite a contrast from the average person. For example, it is a human trait to automatically harbor hatred toward your enemies, but not the Son of God. He said, *"Love your enemies and pray for those who persecute you"* (Matthew 5:44).

> **"Love Your Enemies and Pray for Those Who Persecute You."**
> – *Matthew 5:44*

You may say, "Is that even possible? How can I ever respond like that?"

Believe Jesus when He says you can think as He thinks – and even more. He declared, *"Verily, verily, I say unto you, He that believeth on me, the works that I do shall he do also; and greater works than these shall he do; because I go unto my Father"* (John 14:12 KJV).

This is attainable because He has given us His Spirit.

Is it Possible?

Most people don't have a problem accepting the

fact that Jesus was the Son of God, yet they do have trouble believing they can be just like Him – and achieve the things He accomplished.

They admit, "I believe Christ came so that we could go to heaven," but they forget He was sent to earth that we might experience overcoming power. Jesus tells us *"with God all things are possible"* (Mark 10:27). And John, the beloved disciple, wrote, *"As he is, so are we in this world"* (1John 4:17 KJV).

Jesus is everything we should strive to become.

SMASH THE MOLD!

One characteristic of Christ that stands out to me is the fact that regardless of the critics, He was not about to compromise His calling to be accepted.

Heroes break barriers. If you are not careful, those around you will try to confine you in a box from which you can't escape. It should be your objective to smash the mold!

Jesus did not casually go with the flow – He *was* the flow!

Before the Son of God appeared on the scene, the Almighty had been silent for more than 400 years. Obviously the old traditions just weren't working! Jesus began His public ministry by announcing a new agenda. He boldly stated: *"Repent, for the kingdom of heaven is near"* (Matthew 4:17).

Christ was declaring the fulfilment of Old Testament prophecy. Through Isaiah, God said, *"Forget the former things; do not dwell on the past. See, I am doing a new thing! Now it springs up; do you not perceive it? I am making a way in the desert and streams in the wasteland"* (Isaiah 43:18-19).

Praise God! Our dry, thirsty days are history!

NO LIMIT LIVING!

When you carefully study the life of Jesus, you'll find He spent much of His ministry dealing with the traditions of man. That's worth noting. If the Lord was not restricted by patterns and practices, neither should you.

> *DON'T BECOME BOGGED DOWN IN A RUT OF YOUR OWN MAKING – START CUTTING A NEW PATH.*

To take a giant leap forward, step out in faith and attempt something new. Don't become bogged down in a rut of your own making – start cutting a new path.

SHAKING UP THE SYSTEM

When our *Full Turn* ministry began we broke a few religious traditions – at least it seemed that way by the

ONLY A MAN WHO KNOWS
WHAT IT IS LIKE TO BE DEFEATED
CAN REACH DOWN TO THE
BOTTOM OF HIS SOUL AND COME
UP WITH THE EXTRA OUNCE OF
POWER IT TAKES TO WIN WHEN
THE MATCH IS EVEN.

– MUHAMMAD ALI

verbal abuse we took from those who were upset and shocked by change.

I can honestly say I wasn't trying to be offensive or rebellious; only following God's directive into new areas.

Don't misunderstand. I know some traditions are necessary and based on the Word of God. However, we were breaking free from the man-made routines I was convinced the Lord never intended for us to have.

THROUGH THE CENTURIES THE WORLD HASN'T CHANGED. PEOPLE STILL WANT TO STEREOTYPE WHAT THEY DON'T UNDERSTAND.

My strength came from knowing that Jesus endured similar criticism. The religious leaders of His day called Him a *"winebibber"* and *"a friend of publicans and sinners"* (Matthew 11:19).

Why was He so reviled? He was shaking up the system – breaking down tradition.

Through the centuries the world hasn't changed. People still want to stereotype what they don't understand. They reject everyone whose culture is not in the image of theirs – announcing, "Here are the boundaries and woe be to anyone who starts coloring outside the lines."

GO AHEAD!

Listen to the Lord when He proclaims, *"As the heavens are higher than the earth, so are my ways higher than your ways and my thoughts than your thoughts"* (Isaiah 55:9)

Yes, people are going to gossip and talk, but that doesn't mean you are required to listen. I smile when I see those who once lashed out against our ministry now attempting to duplicate our programs. Instead of being angry, I rejoice – after all, blazing a trail is what being a pioneer is all about.

The sky is the limit to your future if you are not afraid to follow in God's footsteps. Go ahead – break a few barriers!

TAKE A BOLD LEAP FORWARD

Heroes aren't cowards. The lion did not earn the title "King of the jungle" for no good reason – he aggressively stakes out his territory and often defends it to the death.

That's what God expects of His children. Solomon wrote: *"The wicked man flees though no one pursues, but the righteous are as bold as a lion"* (Proverbs 28:1).

Who needs to run and hide? Only the wicked – for they have no assurance of tomorrow or an anchor for their soul. However, if you are in Christ you have an expectation that reaches far beyond the natural. And that gives us confidence. As Paul expresses it: *"Therefore, since we have such a hope, we are very bold"* (2 Corinthians 3:12).

Become assertive in your pursuit of the prize. In

When I was in the Batter's Box, I Felt Sorry for the Pitcher!

– Roger Hornsby

the skirmishes and conflicts that always come, decide to run *toward* the battle instead of away from it – knowing God is fighting by your side.

START EXERCISING!

The Lord has a fantastic workout program! The Word tells us to *"be strong in the Lord and in his mighty power"* (Ephesians 6:10).

What kind of might are we talking about? Oh, I believe God can strengthen our mortal bodies – He proved that through Samson. What we need, however is an inward strength that builds our heart, soul and mind.

> *IF YOU WANT TO BE SPIRITUALLY "FIT," START EXERCISING YOUR FAITH.*

If you want to be spiritually "fit," start exercising your faith – your ability to believe and hold onto the promise. Faith is *"substance"* (Hebrews 11:1) – or the *stuff* – that produces the unquenchable desire to excel.

We exercise our faith by *trying* it (James 1:3).

STEP OUT OF THE BOAT!

Do you remember the story of Jesus walking on the water? The disciples were afraid and thought what was

GO TO THE ANT...CONSIDER ITS WAYS AND BE WISE! IT HAS NO COMMANDER, NO OVERSEER OR RULER, YET IT STORES ITS PROVISIONS IN SUMMER AND GATHERS ITS FOOD AT HARVEST.

– PROVERBS 6:6-8

coming toward them in the storm was a ghost, or some kind of spirit.

The Lord must have smiled when He saw the frightened men. Simon Peter said to Him, *"Lord, if it's you...tell me to come to you on the water"* (Matthew 14:28).

At that point he *tried* his faith – by stepping out of the boat and walking on the waves like Jesus. Yet, when his eyes focused on the wind and the storm he began to sink.

Many ridicule Peter for his lack of total faith, but at least he ventured out of the vessel. Remember, there were eleven other disciples on board who had the same opportunity to walk on the water, yet they were too afraid to try.

Peter was building his faith – preparing for a time when he would need it even more.

You are anchored in Christ. Don't be fearful of stepping out of the boat!

"HOW DARE YOU!"

Jesus was never timid when it came to speaking the truth.

During the time of the Jewish Passover, He went to the temple courts in Jerusalem and found men selling cattle, sheep and doves – and others sitting at tables

A GOOD PLAN VIOLENTLY
EXECUTED RIGHT NOW IS FAR
BETTER THAN A PERFECT PLAN
EXECUTED NEXT WEEK.

– GEORGE S. PATTON

exchanging money.

Jesus surveyed the scene and became outraged – no longer the meek, mild person many thought Him to be. Scripture records that *"he made a whip out of cords, and drove all from the temple area, both sheep and cattle; he scattered the coins of the money changers and overturned their tables"* (John 2:15).

To those selling doves and livestock, Jesus commanded: *"Get these out of here! How dare you turn my Father's house into a market!"* (v.16).

DON'T BACK DOWN

There are situations in life when a passive attitude won't suffice. You must speak the truth – regardless of what others may think, or the consequences.

YOU WILL NEVER KNOW VICTORY UNTIL YOU ARE WILLING TO ENGAGE IN THE FIGHT OF FAITH.

You will never know victory until you are willing to engage in the fight of faith.

Don't back down from the challenge of your dream. Instead, embrace your vision and run with total confidence into the fray knowing *"we are more than conquerors through him who loved us"* (Romans 8:37).

133

NEW COURAGE

After the outpouring of the Spirit in the Upper Room, the believers began to proclaim the message of Christ with amazing authority. It shook society to such an extent that Peter and John were thrown in jail, then called before the high priests and elders of the day. The clerics demanded to know, *"By what power or what name did you do this?"* (Acts 4:7).

The Spirit-filled disciples proclaimed Christ, saying *"there is no other name under heaven given to men by which we must be saved"* (v.12).

The Bible records: *"Now when they saw the boldness of Peter and John, and perceived that they were unlearned and ignorant men, they marveled; and they took knowledge of them, that they had been with Jesus"* (Acts 4:13 KJV).

Following their release, Peter and John called the believers together to rejoice at what the Lord was doing. *"After they prayed, the place where they were meeting was shaken. And they were all filled with the Holy Spirit and spoke the word of God boldly"* (Acts 4:31)

Ask the Lord to fortify you with His daring and courage. Remember, your leader is the Lion of the Tribe of Judah!

STEP 17

YOU *ARE* A HERO!

As a kid I loved to watch a certain cartoon about ordinary, everyday objects that could magically transform themselves into heroes who saved the day.

For example, there was a car on one show that could change itself into a fighting robot – with amazing power and agility.

It may sound far-fetched, but let's put this into the context of what we've been discussing.

To some, Jesus was just the son of Joseph and Mary – a carpenter by trade who was brought up in Nazareth, a city people of the day didn't hold in high regard. The Bible says, "*He was in the world, and though the world was made through him, the world did not recognize him*" (John 1:10).

People viewed Jesus as average – just another nobody claiming to be somebody.

WITHOUT THE ASSISTANCE OF A DIVINE BEING, I CANNOT SUCCEED. WITH THAT ASSISTANCE, I CANNOT FAIL.

– ABRAHAM LINCOLN

They failed to recognize this same Man was the Son of God, and could not see the Spirit within which gave Him such ability.

GREAT CHANGES!

On the surface, a hero may look like every other person, but what is hidden inside transforms them into something far more.

Without the anointing of God, the best you can expect is mediocrity. Yet, when His Spirit is alive and working inside you, a marvelous conversion begins – and you are changed into the likeness of Christ.

> *WITHOUT THE ANOINTING OF GOD, THE BEST YOU CAN EXPECT IS MEDIOCRITY.*

The apostle Paul said, *"And we, who with unveiled faces all reflect the Lord's glory, are being transformed into his likeness with ever-increasing glory, which comes from the Lord, who is the Spirit"* (2 Corinthians 3:18).

A new you is possible!

- We are conformed to His likeness (Romans 8:29).
- The Father will *"transform our lowly bodies*

MAY HE GIVE YOU THE DESIRE OF YOUR HEART AND MAKE ALL YOUR PLANS SUCCEED.

– PSALM 20:4

so that they will be like his glorious body" (Philippians 3:21).

- *"When he appears, we shall be like him, for we shall see him as he is"* (1 John 3:2).

As a caterpillar enters a cocoon and later emerges as a butterfly, we also must enter into the Spirit of Christ to become children of God. Regardless of what you yearn to be, He can provide the power to become.

> *REGARDLESS OF WHAT YOU YEARN TO BE, HE CAN PROVIDE THE POWER TO BECOME.*

SUPERCHARGED!

Sadly, because of today's crime rates, many policemen are forced to use "stun guns." They are powered only by a 9-volt battery, capable of passing 45,000 volts of electricity through an impending attacker. The battery itself will do little damage – you might press it to your tongue and only get a little tickle. But let that power be placed in the stun gun and it is suddenly converted into high voltage.

I give this example to emphasize that when we are in Christ, we are changed into people of power – supercharged, ready to take on any challenge. No

GOD IS PREPARING HIS HEROES; AND WHEN THE OPPORTUNITY COMES, HE CAN FIT THEM INTO THEIR PLACES IN A MOMENT, AND THE WORLD WILL WONDER WHERE THEY CAME FROM.

– A. B. SIMPSON

longer are we forced to rely on our ordinary ability. What He gives us is extraordinary!

Jesus said, *"You will receive power when the Holy Spirit comes on you"* (Acts 1:8).

YOUR SOURCE OF CONFIDENCE

Today, and every day that follows, see yourself in a different light. Instead of saying, "It might happen," you can declare, "I am determined! Nothing will stop me from victory!"

This is not about being filled with pride and arrogance, rather being confident in the ability God has given you – and moving forward in that calling.

> *EVEN THOUGH THE WORLD MAY NOT YET RECOGNIZE THE FACT, IN YOUR FATHER'S SIGHT YOU ARE A HERO.*

Far too long we have believed the words of a song "For such a worm as I." Let me reassure you that as a believer, you are no longer a *worm*. You are a cherished child of the Most High God.

"I AM!"

Even though the world may not yet recognize the fact, in your Father's sight you are a hero.

I am what God says I am! – a conqueror, an overcomer, a victor, a champion. Why should I be ashamed of something that God gave me the ability and the right to say?

If you truly believe Jesus is your King and has given you authority over all things, you will begin to live and act with that assurance. Because Christ has dominion – we have dominion. Since He has overcome the world – so can we.

Go ahead and proclaim it: "Because He is, I am!"

- "I am blessed!"
- "I am at peace!"
- "I am filled with joy!"
- "I am strong!"

Please know that I am praying with you as you put these 17 steps into practice. As a result of your vision, your spirit and your diligence, I believe you will one day stand before God as one of His treasured heroes.

Well done!

FOR A COMPLETE LIST OF BOOKS
AND TAPES BY THE AUTHOR
OR TO SCHEDULE HIM FOR SPEAKING
ENGAGEMENTS, CONTACT:

ALAN MUSHEGAN, JR.
FULL TURN MINISTRIES
1521 HURT ROAD
MARIETTA, GA 30008

PHONE: 770-435-1152
INTERNET: www.fullturn.com
EMAIL: ft@fullturn.com